CAREERS *in Your Community*™

WORKING *as a* PHYSICAL THERAPIST *in* YOUR COMMUNITY

David Kassnoff

ROSEN
PUBLISHING®

New York

Published in 2016 by The Rosen Publishing Group, Inc.
29 East 21st Street, New York, NY 10010

First Edition

Library of Congress Cataloging-in-Publication Data

Kassnoff, David, author.
Working as a physical therapist in your community/David Kassnoff.—First edition.
     pages cm.—(Careers in your community)
Audience: Grades 7 to 8.
Includes bibliographical references and index.
ISBN 978-1-4994-6109-1 (library bound)
1. Physical therapy—Vocational guidance—Juvenile literature. 2. Physical therapists—Juvenile literature. I. Title.
RM705.K37 2016
615.8'2023–dc23

                                                                    2014045157

Manufactured in the United States of America

Contents

Introduction

Who needs a physical therapist in your community? The fitness-minded neighbor who jogs every day and injures his knee does. The great-grandmother who takes a fall on a slippery front step does. The fifth-grade student who has been screened by a school physician and diagnosed with scoliosis does, too. The office worker who is recovering from a shoulder injury and needs to go back to work does. So does the basketball player who wants to return to the court quickly after an injury. The proud military veteran determined to walk in a Memorial Day parade despite suffering from chronic pain from a battle wound does, too.

Physical therapists in your community help these people, and many more like them, every day. They bring years of education to the job of helping people regain their ability to walk, run, work, and play. They also bring an array of problem-solving skills because physical therapists often need to teach a patient's family how to act as caregivers and coaches once the patient is back home.

Like most health care professionals, physical therapists need more than a college education and internships. They must develop physical, mental, and emotional stamina, too. They often find themselves

Physical therapists use a variety of exercises and encouragement to help people regain their strength and mobility. Sometimes, a simple elastic band is effective and easy for patients to use.

down on the floor, helping patients with stretching exercises. Physical therapists also need to figure out ways to convince stubborn patients to take part in specific exercises. They must put in extra effort whenever a patient is gloomy.

Does this sounds like hard work? Most physical therapists would agree that every day brings fresh challenges. But they do the work anyway—in hospitals, in schools, in nursing facilities, in sports training rooms, and in people's homes—because every physical therapist knows he or she is making a positive difference in a person's life. A therapist gets to know a patient's moods, joys, and doubts. There is a strong emotional payback when a patient returns to an active lifestyle, and strong bonds can form between the patient and therapist.

Physical therapy involves using exercises, massage, manipulation, and other techniques to help patients regain their abilities. These practices date back to the 1500s in Europe, and in the 1800s, exercise and muscle reeducation were widely used. The polio epidemic of 1916 prompted renewed use of muscle testing and muscle reeducation.

In 1918, World War I led the U.S. Army to organize the first training classes in physical therapy for "reconstruction aides" to work in army hospitals. At the Boston School of Physical Education, groups of students were trained in six-week courses, and women then known as medical therapists learned the basics of what would later become physiotherapy.

As physical therapy grew, more training opportunities became available, and states established standards for education and licensing. Today, more than two hundred thousand physical therapists work in the United States, usually caring for patients as part of a team of doctors, nurses, and other health care professionals, while others work independently from physicians.

Physical therapy is a rewarding way to help all types of people throughout your community. It's often hard work, requiring persistence and patience—but it can be a very rewarding career path.

CHAPTER One

By the Numbers

Each year, about nine million Americans receive outpatient physical therapy services, as physical therapy in a therapist's office, fitness center, sports facility, or other nonhospital location is known. Why is there a strong demand for physical therapists and physical therapy assistants? The simple answer is that people are living longer and, in some cases, retiring earlier to try sports and pursuits they've put off in their working years. Also, as older people recover from joint replacements or injuries, they require physical therapy to help regain their ability to live normally. Many health science breakthroughs are helping people live longer, and this means an increased need for physical therapists and physical therapy assistants to treat older citizens whose bodies become frail as they age.

Most health care providers recommend regular exercise to help patients avoid health problems. Sometimes, overexercising and injuries can lead to an unexpected visit to the doctor. About 108 million Americans age eighteen or older experienced a musculoskeletal injury in 2005—from a dislocated shoulder to a muscle tear—that lasted longer than three months. That's about half the over-eighteen population.

In 2007 alone, patients and/or their health insurers paid about $13.5 billion for some eighty-eight million ambulatory (nonhospitalized) physical therapy visits.

For many people, the appeal of newer exercises such as inline skating may result in a need for physical therapy to help recover from muscle strains or mild injuries.

This demonstrates the huge demand for physical therapists to help rehabilitate people recovering from injuries, accidents, and chronic pain situations.

Meeting the Demand

Physical therapists care for people of all ages and in various degrees of health. This requires a physical therapist to bring a positive attitude, warm and friendly personality, and the ability to offer imaginative ways to persuade patients to try new exercises and stick to a rehabilitation plan. A willingness to listen to opinions of other health care team members is important, too. A successful physical therapist feels confident working with patients of different ages, genders, and backgrounds. Kindness is essential. Hugs, praise, and high-fives are always welcome.

As amateur and professional athletes train and compete, they need conditioning exercises to strengthen their muscles and recover from on-the-field injuries. For example, when the National Football League (NFL) and the NFL Players Association signed their 2013 collective bargaining agreement, the contract required each of the NFL's thirty-two teams to employ at least one full-time physical therapist. Those therapists must be certified specialists in sports physical therapy to help players rebound from injuries suffered in practice and during games.

Even in male-dominated pro sports, physical therapy isn't an all-boys' club. In late 2011, the L.A. Dodgers of Major League Baseball appointed Sue Falsone as the first female athletic head trainer in one of the four major U.S. pro sports (baseball, basketball, football, and hockey). Falsone holds a

When a pro athlete suffers an injury in practice, preseason, or during a game, a sports physical therapist provides one-on-one attention to help a player recover without further injury.

bachelor's degree in physical therapy from Daemen College in Amherst, New York, and a master's degree in human movement science and sports medicine from the University of North Carolina at Chapel Hill.

Such glass ceilings are shattered, in part, because more women are training to become physical therapists today. The American Physical Therapy Association (APTA) has more than seventy-two thousand members and reports that nearly 70 percent of its members are women. About 74 percent of all licensed physical therapists are women. Females outnumber males enrolled in educational programs to become licensed practitioners

OUR AGING MUSCLES

When adults complain about "feeling the chill in their bones," there is a reason. As people age, musculoskeletal problems—ailments and diseases involving weakened bones and muscles—occur. People who are sixty-five and older account for 12 to 13 percent of the total population. By 2030, seniors will make up 20 percent of the population, an increase of more than 50 percent. Adults don't always age well; activities that wear on bones and joints in younger years, a sedentary lifestyle, and obesity all can contribute to joint diseases. Many seniors expect to enjoy active lives in their retirement years, but they will need more health care services, including physical therapy, to deal with musculoskeletal diseases.

by about three to one. About twenty thousand students enroll in the more than two hundred physical therapy programs in the United States each year.

In Canada, about 77 percent of all physiotherapists are female. Canada's future physical therapists study for their bachelor's degrees in physiotherapy at thirteen universities across the country.

A Growing Field

There are around 204,000 physical therapists working in the profession today, and the U.S. Bureau of Labor Statistics says that number will grow in the next

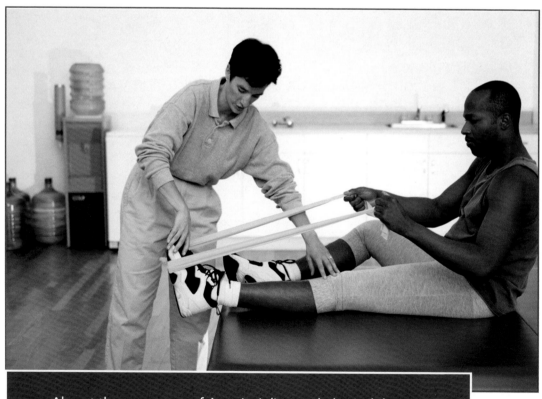

Almost three-quarters of America's licensed physical therapists are female, and they work with both male and female patients in need of exercises, therapies, and manipulation.

decade. In fact, by 2022, the agency expects another 73,500 people to become physical therapists. Because physical therapists are in demand, these are usually well-paying jobs that offer the opportunity to work with a variety of people and not be tied to a desk in an office.

What about salary? The Bureau of Labor Statistics tracks up-to-date salary information that shows the range of salaries for physical therapists. It is a well-paying career in general, depending on the therapist's experience and whether he or she works for a large regional health system or chooses to be self-employed.

Other factors influence salary, too. A newly graduated physical therapist will likely earn less at the start of his or her career than an experienced physical therapist. Salaries are also affected by location, whether a therapist supervises others, and if the therapist has an area of specialization that is in high demand.

CHAPTER Two

What a Physical Therapist Does

When a patient visits a physical therapist for the first time, he or she is probably recovering from an injury or medical procedure, such as a knee replacement. It is up to the physical therapist to examine that individual, study notes provided by the patient's doctor and other professionals, and develop a plan of care.

The goal is to help a patient find ways to regain his or her ability to move and function, reduce pain, and prevent disability. Physical therapists, or PTs, also work with individuals—and sometimes, with their family members—to develop fitness and wellness programs for healthier and more active lifestyles. These activities can help prevent loss of mobility and often enable a patient to function normally.

Physical therapists are doctors, too. To become a practicing physical therapist in the United States today, a physical therapist must earn a Doctor of Physical Therapy (DPT) degree, pass the National Physical Therapy Examination (NPTE), and obtain a license to practice physical therapy in his or her state.

All About Care

Physical therapists have a number of roles. They diagnose patients' dysfunctional movements by methods such as observing them stand or walk and listening to their concerns. A physical therapist will set up a plan of care for each patient, outlining the patient's goals and the expected outcome of the plan. The PT will also use exercises, stretching maneuvers, hands-on therapy, and equipment to ease patients' pain, help them increase their mobility, prevent further pain or injury, and facilitate health and wellness. Another important part of a physical therapist's job is to evaluate the patient's progress, modifying a plan of care and trying new treatments as needed.

But physical therapists don't act alone. First, they consult with physicians, nurses, and other health care professionals. They view documents called referrals, provided by doctors and surgeons, which describe the patient's original symptoms, a diagnosis, and the course of treatment taken by the medical team. These reports may offer suggestions for ways that a physical therapist can help rehabilitate a patient who has completed a treatment process, a surgical procedure, or other course of treatment.

Often, a good physical therapist will go beyond the documents to ask for more details. Some doctor-PT conversations take place by phone, but others prefer face-to-face discussions. Sometimes, doctors rely on physical therapists to evaluate patients who've had joint-replacement surgery to test if the patient can stand and move well enough to be discharged from a hospital.

An important skill for a therapist is listening! Even when doctors provide reports about their patients, conversations between patient and therapist are a necessity.

Looking and Listening

No two patients—or their treatments—are alike. Some are comfortable being touched during a physical therapist's evaluation, while others resist physical contact with the therapist. As a result, the work of physical therapists varies by the type of patient.

How a therapist decides to treat a patient is very important. A physical therapist needs to diagnose patients' dysfunctional movements by observing them stand or walk and by listening to their concerns. Physical therapists watch for hesitancy and listen for when a patient's voice changes while describing his or her pains. At the same time, the physical therapist needs to ask thoughtful questions and be a good communicator.

For example, a patient recovering from a stroke may experience difficulty moving afterward. He or she may be frustrated by a loss of motor skills, or even the ability to speak well. This requires a physical therapist to create a different care plan for a stroke patient than he or she might draw up for an athlete recovering from a knee injury.

Tools of Physical Therapy

Carpenters use specialized tools to build houses. Artists use different brushes and canvas materials to create their works of art. So it's no surprise that physical therapists rely on a select variety of tools, equipment, and computer software to perform their jobs. Balance beams or boards, bolsters, and rockers are used in the rehabilitation or therapy process. So are treadmills, assistive walking devices, and exercise balls. Pivotal

Physical therapists sometimes suggest using an upper-body ergometer. It can help patients regain strength in their arms, shoulders, and surrounding muscle groups.

traction therapy supplies include cervical pivots, lumbar pivots, occipivots, and thoracic pivots. Patients lie on these molded forms to treat soft tissue around the spine. Physical therapists test patients' reflexes with reflex hammers. A resistance shoulder wheel is used for exercises to strengthen the shoulder, arm, and wrist. An upper-body ergometer measures the work upper-body muscles are doing and is often used by people recovering from shoulder injuries or surgery. Patients lie or sit on a range of traction and mobilization physical therapy tables. PTs also use instruments that measure a range of motion, including digital inclinometers,

DRAMATIC RECOVERIES

Moviemakers have often featured physical therapy as a plot device in their films. A few of these features include *Born on the Fourth of July* (a 1989 film about Vietnam War veteran Ron Kovic), *Murderball* (a 2005 documentary about paraplegics in wheelchair basketball), *The Diving Bell and the Butterfly* (a 2007 film about a paralyzed magazine editor), *Warm Springs* (a 2005 HBO film about future president Franklin D. Roosevelt), and the 1994 comedy *Muriel's Wedding*. One film—2010's *Just Wright*—features Queen Latifah as a physical therapist who tries to help a pro basketball player recover from an injury.

electronic manual muscle testers, and muscle testing equipment. They rely on devices to help evaluate patients' perceptual, sensory, or dexterity abilities.

For technology, physical therapists use a variety of computer software to help evaluate patients' abilities, write up treatment reports, and manage their practices. These include specialized medical therapy software, biometrics video games, and programs to help document rehabilitation progress, as well as accounting and word-processing software.

Helping patients in your community deal with their pain is a process that continues after a physical therapist makes a diagnosis. Over the course of many weeks, a physical therapist will ask about the patient's level of pain during and after each session, as well as between sessions. By prescribing home exercises and using a skeletal model to show a patient where the exercises have the most effect, the PT helps patients deal with their pain on the road to recovery.

Overcoming Frustrations

Seeing patients progress from limited mobility to regaining their strength and movement is a joyous moment for any physical therapist. Not every patient makes a complete recovery, however, and some patients face setbacks and become discouraged. When patients become discouraged or frustrated with a lack of progress, they may become angry or discontinue rehabilitation. This is most likely with older adults or patients with long-term injuries, such as military veterans.

For a physical therapist, it is challenging to step back from a patient whose rehabilitation isn't

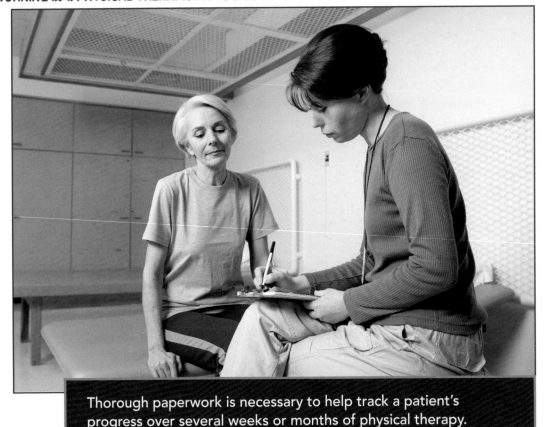

Thorough paperwork is necessary to help track a patient's progress over several weeks or months of physical therapy. Insurers and doctors need to review these documents.

complete. There is an emotional investment, as well as the physical requirements of working with each patient, that may create a bond that is hard to disconnect. For all the patience and encouragement the PT offers, not every patient regains mobility or independence.

An entirely different form of frustration comes from the paperwork that every physical therapist must manage. Careful records for each patient's progress are expected, as health insurance companies demand detailed documentation. In addition, a new, global set of diagnoses and treatment codes known as ICD-10 are designed to help track health issues in sharper detail. Physical therapists need to understand these detailed coding systems when documenting diagnoses and be aware of how they are used in their patient paperwork.

While there are moments of achievement and reward in the life of a physical therapist, those moments will be offset by patient setbacks and paperwork chores that no one enjoys. Learn to cherish the rewarding moments to help balance any frustrations.

CHAPTER Three

PTs in the Workplace

Physical therapists are perhaps the most mobile health care workers. They can find work in a variety of settings, from an outpatient center to a sports training complex to a hospital. Depending on the clients and patients they serve, they can find themselves working in several different locations over the work week.

For example, a physical therapist specializing in pediatric medicine can find himself or herself visiting several public schools, a child care center, and the pediatric department of a community hospital to assess and treat young patients. A sports medicine PT may have an unusual schedule, working with athletes at a team's practice facility some days and accompanying the team on a road trip at other times.

Seniors and elderly patients receive treatment in various locations, including hospitals, extended care facilities, rehabilitation clinics, and their homes. Some PTs specialize in one type of care, such as orthopedics or geriatrics. Many physical therapists also work at preventing loss of mobility by developing fitness and wellness programs to encourage healthier and more active lifestyles.

Where PTs Meet Patients

Hospitals, extended care facilities, nursing homes, and skilled nursing facilities are often operated by regional health care systems that manage multiple buildings and staffs. At these facilities, patients may spend long periods in bed, resulting in a loss of strength or movement. In these settings, a physical therapy director may lead a staff of therapists. In smaller, rural hospitals, a single physical therapist may serve both the hospital and nearby nursing

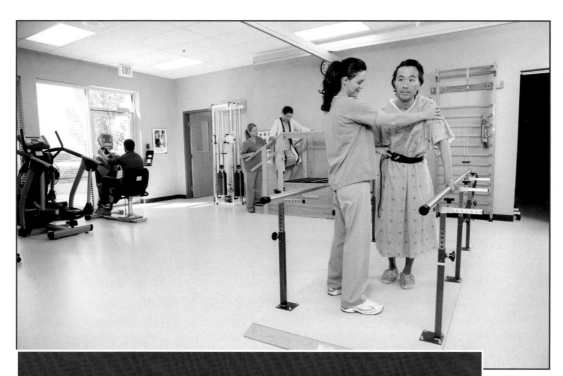

Physical therapists must become experts in the use of a variety of equipment, from simple parallel bars to electronically controlled fitness machines.

homes. It is also not unusual to find physical therapists working in an emergency room, helping ER staff diagnose and treat dislocations and wounds.

Outpatient clinics and doctor's offices may function as private practice groups or be privately owned or run by a practice management company. Some practices are owned and operated by hospitals. These clinics and groups serve patients who are mobile and can live at home. Physical therapists help these patients deal with pain management after surgery or injury, cope with chronic illness such as arthritis or cerebral palsy, and regain their strength while recuperating at home.

A popular trend in medicine today is urgent care offices that bridge the gap between hospitals and doctors' offices. In an urgent care facility, walk-in patients can be evaluated for minor injuries and ailments without a visit to the emergency room. Depending on the organization, some urgent care centers provide physical therapy services during regular business hours.

At schools and preschools, the school staff may call in a physical therapist to evaluate a student's ability to move independently in classroom or physical education activities. Some schools have PTs that specialize in pediatric medicine on their staffs. A school physical therapist focuses on a child's ability to move as independently as possible in school. The PT evaluates the child's ability to move throughout the school and take part in classroom activities.

Fitness and wellness centers rely on physical therapists to guide the rehabilitation and strength training of their members. So do sports teams. Sports medicine is a popular specialty, as many colleges and

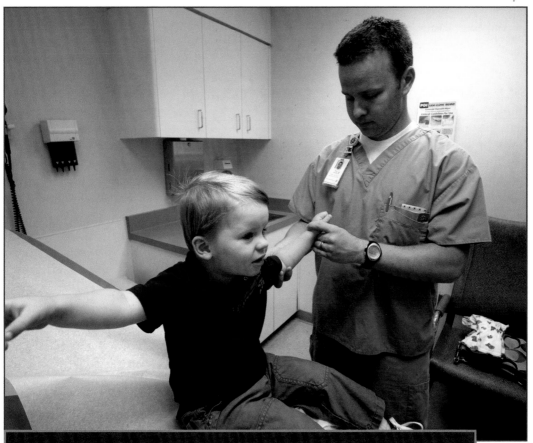

Schools often ask physical therapists to work with young children with poor walking or motor skills. Treating these problems early can help students avoid long-term issues later on.

universities have growing athletic programs to attract undergraduates.

Patients needing in-home health delivery can ask a home health agency to send a nearby physical therapist when they are unable to travel. In the home, a physical therapist can evaluate the patient's mobility needs, such as how far the patient needs to walk between rooms, or whether there are outdoor areas—a yard or nearby park—where the patient could try different therapies or exercises.

NOT A DESK JOB

Heidi Bechtold, a physical therapist in western New York State, specializes in pediatric care. She loves that her workplace changes every day. "Thank God I don't have a desk job," she says of her schedule visiting homes and schools to see young patients. "Every day of the week is different, and that means I have to be organized." She enjoys working with children and sets her schedule so that she works a full week over four days. She sees about six children each day. "The best part of my job is that I can make a positive difference in each person's life," says Bechtold.

Choosing a Place

Some physical therapists work in more traditional workplaces, such as factories, military bases, research centers, or factories. Depending on the organization's needs, these therapists can help address employees' problems with ergonomics, repetitive motion disorders, or muscle strains from overexertion.

Physical therapists who like a variety of workplaces may set up their own private practices. By networking with medical professionals in their communities, they can agree to provide services to doctors' groups, home health care agencies, and private clients. They go where the patients' needs take them.

In almost all these workplaces, physical therapists must create treatment methods—called modalities—built around therapeutic exercise and functional training. Depending on the needs of a given patient, PTs may "mobilize" a joint or massage a muscle to improve movement and function. They may use other techniques, such as electrotherapy, ultrasound (high-frequency waves that create heat), and other measures.

"You need to be ingenious, sometimes," says Denise Lippa, a physical therapist in Rochester, New York. "If you're doing home care, for example, you may be dealing with patients who are obese or elderly, and getting them to move can be difficult." She describes using a variety of household items to help motivate patients, including raising a couch in an obese patient's home to make it easier for the patient to rise from a seated position.

CHAPTER Four

Becoming a Physical Therapist

With more than two hundred universities and training programs for physical therapy in the United States and Canada, students have plenty of ways to pursue a physical therapy career. But the education requirements to become a physical therapist have changed in recent years.

Before College

As is the case with most health-related professions, a good foundation in science and math is extremely important. These subjects will help students understand how the human body works, as well as how principles of basic physics apply to the therapies used to help patients recover and rehabilitate themselves.

No less important, however, is finding opportunities to observe physical therapists at work. Volunteering to help out your school's athletic trainer can provide a close-up look at what a physical therapist does. Nursing homes and child care centers in your community may also offer volunteer opportunities that will give you a chance to watch physical therapists in action.

Volunteering in a rehabilitation center enables teenagers to shadow physical therapists and decide if physical therapy is a career they wish to pursue.

Volunteering will help students decide if physical therapy is right for them. They will realize if a career in medicine is a good fit and whether they are comfortable working with many different people. Some therapies can appear repetitive, so a student who is easily bored must realize that repetition is part of the physical therapy regimen.

Lastly, it is important to develop essential qualities that people expect in a health care professional: compassion, attention to detail, flexibility, dexterity, interpersonal skills, and physical stamina.

Bye-Bye, Bachelor's Degree

A few years ago, the requirements for becoming a physical therapist changed. A bachelor's degree from a four-year college or university is no longer enough to become a licensed physical therapist. Instead, a doctor of physical therapy (DPT) degree is now the standard.

However, earning a bachelor's degree in pre-physical therapy, athletic training, biology, or health science will help undergraduates meet the requirements to enroll in physical therapy graduate school. Look for majors such as biology, chemistry, physics, and physiology. A degree program in physical therapist assisting will also prepare students for a graduate degree program.

Some colleges offer accelerated combination programs, such as a six-year program calling for three years at the undergraduate level and three years in a DPT program. In any case, students should expect to study anatomy, chemistry, mathematics, physics, physiology, and psychology.

Students looking to become a physical therapy assistant (PTA) can complete a two-year program—

Understanding human anatomy and physiology are essential, whether a student plans to become a physical therapist or a physical therapy assistant.

sometimes at a community college—and enter the profession. These programs include classroom study and clinical experience and emphasize algebra, English, anatomy, physiology, and psychology. Assistants obtain hands-on experience in treatment centers, and they can earn certifications in cardiopulmonary resuscitation (CPR) and other first-aid skills.

PTAs work under the supervision of a physical therapist and tend to earn somewhat less than PTs. The job outlook for a PTA is strong: the Bureau of Labor Statistics reported more than 121,000 PTA jobs in 2012. It anticipates nearly fifty thousand new positions by 2022.

Finding the Right College

What are the top U.S. physical therapy programs? *U.S. News & World Report* provides rankings of many of the 218 colleges and universities offering these degrees. Its 2012 list of top schools includes the University of Southern California in Los Angeles, University of Delaware in Newark, University of Pittsburgh, Washington University in St. Louis, University of Iowa in Iowa City, U.S. Army-Baylor University, Emory University, MGH Institute of Health Professions, Northwestern University, University of Miami in Coral Gables, University of North Carolina in Chapel Hill, and Marquette University.

In Canada, aspiring PTs can enroll in physiotherapy programs that offer a master's degree and Ph.D. Over a dozen Canadian universities offer master's degrees in physiotherapy. While the majority of these programs

ONLINE PT RECRUITMENT

Want to check out several doctor of physical therapy programs without multiple trips to different universities? The American Physical Therapy Association offers a free, two-day Physical Therapy Virtual Fair on its website. Designed for high school and college students, the fair—held in September—lets students take part in live, online chats with physical therapy programs from across the country and pick up tips on how to get ready to apply to colleges. Remember to visit and register online well before next September's fair.

are taught in English, four of these universities are francophone, or French speaking. Students aiming to become physiotherapist assistants can complete a program at a technical or community college or one at a university.

Choosing a college physical therapy program requires research. A national organization, the Commission on Accreditation in Physical Therapy Education (CAPTE), evaluates college-level PT programs to make sure they meet current standards. In 2013, some 218 programs in the United States and 13 in Canada were recognized as offering accredited programs. Several external websites also provide overall rankings of colleges and universities.

With so many college physical therapy programs to pick from, plan to use online tools offered by professional PT organizations to help find schools and apply for admission.

Narrowing that list to a few preferred schools means involving school counselors and parents in the decision process. The American Physical Therapy Association provides an online tool to assist in evaluating and applying to many—but not all—of these colleges, called a Physical Therapist Centralized Application Service.

What other factors should be weighed? Some students want small class sizes. Tuition and financial aid are important. How far from home do students wish to live? What is the reputation of the faculty and internship opportunities at each school? Does the program provide abundant internship opportunities or career placement assistance? Do the college's location and surrounding community offer volunteer or internship options?

Graduate Education and Beyond

A doctor of physical therapy (DPT) degree is the most-awarded degree from physical therapy programs today. Master's degree programs are also available but are rare. Prior to graduation, students are required to complete a residency under the guidance of an experienced supervisor.

Licensing is the next step. U.S. states require physical therapists to be licensed. Licensing requirements vary from state to state, but most call for a degree from a CAPTE-accredited program and a passing grade on the National Physical Therapy Examination, a five-hour exam that is graded on a scale of 200 to 800. Some states also require continuing education courses to maintain licensure.

Another Path: PT in the Armed Forces

Physical therapy began as a result of battlefield injuries sustained by servicemen in World War I. So it is no surprise that the U.S. Army, Navy, and Air Force—as well as the Canadian armed forces—offer training opportunities for servicemen and servicewomen to become PTs, advance their skills, and pursue job opportunities after completing their military service.

In the army, for example, the Medical Specialist Corps will train its officers to improve soldier readiness by treating them in areas of physical fitness, physical training, and injury prevention. An army PT's responsibilities include providing the military community with neuro-musculoskeletal evaluation, intervention, and case management; performing battlefield Unit Needs Assessments to evaluate mental health status and provide energy conservation assessments; and supervising therapy technicians as they treat soldiers.

To qualify for the U.S. Army's active duty/doctoral program in physical therapy, applicants must have a bachelor's degree in biological sciences, anatomy and physiology, chemistry, physics, social sciences, or statistics. They must also have a qualifying grade point average (GPA) of 3.25 or higher and be between twenty-one and forty years old. The U.S. Navy and Air Force have similar requirements for their physical therapy programs.

Army physical therapists may become eligible for civilian employment after their service in the army has ended by enrolling in the Army PaYS program. This is a recruitment option that guarantees a job

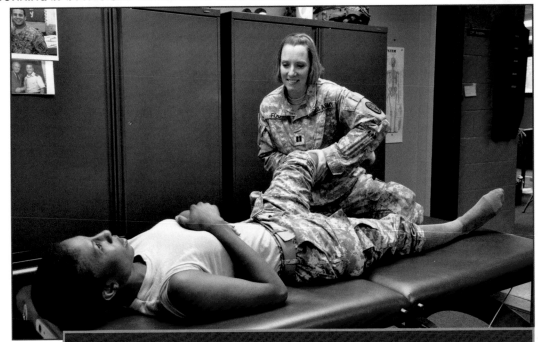

Physical therapists in the armed forces of the United States and Canada help servicemen and servicewomen recover from training and battle injuries.

interview with military-friendly employers looking to recruit experienced and trained veterans.

To become a physiotherapist in the Canadian armed forces, applicants must first complete a fifteen-week basic officer training program at the Canadian Forces Leadership and Recruit School in Quebec. This is followed by a formal preceptorship training for six weeks that provides core administrative knowledge and unique professional information concerning practicing physiotherapy in a military setting. Participants are sent to the Canadian Forces Health Services Training Centre in Borden, Ontario, for a six-week Basic Medical Services Field Course in preparation for future deployments.

CHAPTER *Five*

Searching and Interviewing for PT Jobs

When Kate Zigarowicz was a high school student in Geneva, New York, she became fascinated by the work done by her school's athletic trainer. She also sustained an injury in the summer before her senior year that required rehabilitation. Both events sparked her interest in physical therapy, and she later earned her degree from Daemen College in Buffalo, New York.

After graduation, she became a pediatric PT working with children in Rochester, New York. When she moved to Baltimore, Maryland, finding a job was tougher. "There weren't as many opportunities for pediatrics jobs in Baltimore," she says, "so I took a job in rehabilitation therapy, where I learned a lot of techniques from my team members."

Today, after twelve years as a physical therapist, Zigarowicz still finds joy in her work. "I had a stroke patient whose daughter was getting married in six weeks and wanted to walk his daughter down the aisle," she says. "We worked very hard, he did lots of home exercises with his family, and his daughter was on his arm on her wedding day. You can't beat that feeling."

Changing career paths within physical therapy isn't unusual. Depending on the community, there may be more opportunities in one area of specialization than others. For example, a city with a large school district will often need more pediatric physical therapists than a rural school district with one or two schools. Generally, hospitals with the best rankings for rehabilitation services are in large cities and employ PTs who specialize in rehab skills.

Create a Job Search Plan

Finding a first full-time PT job, or any job, calls for a job search plan. This plan helps map out goals, spell out the tools to compete for a job, organize and keep in touch with professional contacts, and track your progress. Because many jobs are not advertised, a plan reminds the job seeker to network, check multiple resources, and keep résumés and references up-to-date. A job search plan can be handwritten in a paper calendar or set up in a computer program such as Microsoft Word or Excel. It just needs to allow the job seeker to capture names, dates and events, phone numbers, notes, and other key information.

Most job search plans include:

- *Networking*
- *List of target companies/employers*
- *Online job search*
- *Job-related research*
- *Interviewing practice and learning how to answer interview questions*

- *Writing résumés and cover letters*
- *Tailoring a presentation*

While all these are important steps, networking with other physical therapists and health care professionals can help job seekers learn about opportunities before they are posted on a job board or the employer's careers web page.

NETWORKING SECRETS

How do job seekers network? Many local chapters of professional organizations—such as the American Physical Therapy Association—organize mixers, workshops, seminars, and other gatherings. Look for an online chapter's website, LinkedIn page, or Facebook page to find listings in the community. Checking with mentors and coworkers from internships is a good practice, too. Such events all offer get-acquainted opportunities where job seekers can connect with employees in the physical therapy community and ask if they know who is planning to expand their staff.

But networking is not a job fair with snacks and drinks. The purpose of networking is not to hand out copies of a résumé, but to gather and share names, e-mail addresses, and phone numbers of contacts who will know others in the profession. Be prepared by ordering simple business cards that list your name, phone number, and e-mail, as well as the physical therapy role you want. Be ready to share them at any opportunity.

(continued on the next page)

(continued from the previous page)

It is smart to set three realistic goals before attending any networking event. Jot them down on an index card. Keep the goals simple: "Meet three professional contacts who work at City Hospital, the school district, or a day care center" would be an easy goal to achieve at a networking event. Bring a pocket notebook or keep a smartphone handy to capture the name, phone number, and e-mail address of each new connection. Use this information to connect with new contacts on LinkedIn or other social media afterward.

Job Searching via Online Media

APTA's online job listings are one of many sources of potential physical therapy openings. Countless websites—including CareerBuilder.com, Indeed.com, Monster.com, SimplyHired.com, and Glassdoor.com—can be set up to scan websites for physical therapy job listings. Job seekers can post résumés to most of these sites, but be prepared for e-mails and/or phone calls from insurance and financial services companies, who often recruit potential candidates from résumés found on Monster, CareerBuilder, and other job websites.

Hiring experts agree that many stronger job opportunities come from networking than from jobs posted on Indeed or SimplyHired. Why? When a job appears on a regional health system's careers page or Monster.com, the whole world can see it. Through networking, job seekers can learn about an

Online job searches provide information about the skills and experience employers expect from candidates. But networking with other physical therapists can help unearth job openings before they are advertised.

organization's upcoming openings before they appear on a job board—and a fellow alumnus from college or a PT met through networking may be willing to walk a résumé and cover letter to the hiring manager's office on your behalf.

LinkedIn.com is a social media website geared toward professional networking. Look at other physical therapists' LinkedIn profiles as a model for your own. A basic free account, with its online profile and photo, work well. A fee-based premium account gives a little more access to connections, but it isn't necessary. LinkedIn can help a job seeker figure out the connections between contacts at schools, health care organizations, and practices. Job seekers can also post a résumé to LinkedIn.

Are Facebook and Twitter good sites for job seekers? Yes and no. If a job seeker's Facebook friends are mostly other physical therapists and trainers, it's OK to network through them. On Twitter, watch for health care recruiters who post "I'm hiring!" or "Job fair today" tweets; it's worthwhile to follow them to see when new PT opportunities pop up.

Bottom line? Networking can include social media such as LinkedIn and other sites, but job seekers who go out and make face-to-face contact with fellow professionals at networking events can learn about opportunities that don't necessarily appear on job boards.

Choosing a Destination

With many organizations in search of physical therapists and athletic trainers, it is important to have a geographic location in mind. Some new job seekers want to stay near family and friends, while others may wish to

As people live longer, there's a growing demand for physical therapists to help them maintain their strength and flexibility. Working with active seniors can be emotionally satisfying, too.

relocate to a larger community with more opportunities. PT opportunities exist almost everywhere, but therapists who specialize in rehabilitative or nursing home care will find more of those opportunities at universities in warmer regions where many seniors retire. Sports medicine specialists may find plenty of job opportunities in the athletically minded southeastern United States, while pediatric PTs are needed everywhere—but especially in larger cities with big public school systems.

As a start, look at public school systems for PT career opportunities. For example, Wisconsin's public schools employ 280 school-based physical therapists and 40 physical therapist assistants. They serve more than six thousand children receiving school-based physical therapy. Similar statistics can often be found on other states' education department websites. States with higher populations tend to employ more physical therapists in their schools.

If there are too many options, it is smart to network online and in-person with health care employees in your present community. When students have shadowed other PTs and completed internships, the people they have met in these roles can be great contacts for networking.

LinkedIn is a good tool for building professional connections, but so are alumni officers and career development centers at universities offering physical therapy degrees. Their contacts and connections may be willing to introduce job seekers to decision-makers in their workplaces, so add these resources to a job search plan.

Creating a Winning Résumé

No two job descriptions are alike. When writing a résumé, job seekers should note the important skills and experience acquired for a particular job. With those in mind, they should add or subtract details so that the résumé matches the job requirements. Today, career coaches advise that a résumé should be no more than two pages long. The exception to this is when applying for academic or teaching positions, for which candidates often list all their credentials and scholarly publications.

A résumé is not a biography, but really a snapshot of a job seeker's work and education experience that emphasizes how those fit the job opportunity. A recently licensed physical therapist's résumé should capture, in very short bullet points of text, the applicant's:

- *Name, address, contact information, and LinkedIn profile address*
- *College, graduate school, and advanced degrees*
- *Licenses (in which states)*
- *Professional experience in physical therapy, starting with the most recent work or internship*
- *Teaching or mentoring activities*
- *Publications in medical journals or magazines*
- *Research activities*
- *Memberships in professional organizations and any local chapters*
- *Other skills: additional languages, advisory or volunteer roles, etc.*

It is essential to remember that most résumés—even those delivered in person or by a contact within the company—are put through a computerized applicant tracking system. These systems electronically search for keywords in a résumé that match requirements in a particular job description.

For example, a job posting for a physical therapist in Indianapolis says the applicant will "evaluate physician referrals and develop treatment plans; communicate with medical providers about patients and diagnoses," and help create "statistical analysis of the center's therapy performance." To be considered for this job, the job seeker would rewrite his or her résumé to emphasize keywords such as "evaluate referrals, communicate with providers, patients, and statistical analysis."

Most colleges and universities, as well as larger communities, offer workshops and assistance in writing effective résumés. These sessions and advisors can help job seekers polish their résumés so that they get noticed by hiring managers.

A cover letter is a good idea, too. The best cover letters use short sentences to explain why the applicant would be an excellent fit for the job opening and summarize one or two short success stories relating to the applicant's education, work, or internship experience. Save longer stories for the interview. A cover letter should be no more than one single-spaced page.

Thoughtful job seekers use cover letters to demonstrate to hiring managers that they are articulate or that they have noticed an important industry or professional trend. Never address a cover letter to "To Whom It May Concern"; this signals that the applicant has done no research on the company. It is wiser to do some research to find the name and title of a company's recruiter or talent acquisition manager and address the cover letter to that person's attention.

Recruiters and Agencies

Most job fairs are staffed by recruiters from companies that are looking to directly hire workers and by representatives from recruiting agencies that help larger businesses find good candidates. Both perform a kind of harvesting, using a few moments of conversation to decide whether a job seeker's training, attitude, and background match what a hiring manager wants. Recruiters always ask to see résumés. Many will give potential candidates instructions on how to submit their résumés to an online applicant tracking system. It is wise to always

At a job fair, tell recruiters what you do and what job experience you offer. Print up simple business cards with your name, e-mail address, and phone number.

ask the recruiter for his or her business card. These can help job seekers connect with the recruiter later on for future job opportunities.

At the Interview

If a hiring manager likes a candidate's résumé, it can lead to an interview. When offered an interview opportunity, job seekers have a chance to impress the hiring manager. So preparation is essential. Start by researching the company through its website, as well as sites like Glassdoor.com and LinkedIn, to understand the business and its clients.

Job interviews are about sharing information that shows the manager your skills. Making eye contact and sharing short stories about how you help solve workplace problems are important.

When interviewing for a PT position, candidates may meet a series of decision makers one at a time. They might also face a panel in a group interview. In a hospital or clinical organization, expect to meet a director of rehabilitation, director of nursing, other physical therapists, as well as a recruiting or talent acquisition manager. Expect to be asked not only about your education, but also about your experience dealing with conflict in difficult situations.

Most good general interviewing tips apply to interviews for PT jobs, too. For example, remember to bring extra résumés. Dress professionally, be positive, make eye contact, and show confidence without bragging. Be prepared to ask good questions about the company, the challenges it has encountered, and what the interviewer likes most about working there. Don't ask about salary; it's up to the potential employer to raise that topic. It's also a good idea to have a salary range in mind based on salary information available on Glassdoor and other websites, rather than a hard number. Be ready to offer references (the names and phone numbers of professors, internship supervisors, and coworkers). Write thank-you notes to the hiring manager and others in the interview process to help stay on their radar after the interview.

Experienced job seekers will plan ahead for an interview by writing out a few STAR stories—short, one-minute stories that illustrate a work situation, the action the candidate took, and the result. The acronym "STAR" comes from the words "situation, task, activity, result." You will need to make sure your story contains each of these elements. The situation sets the context for the story. For example, an applicant might say, "We were asked to evaluate all the children in a rural elementary school, and the school physician didn't provide background documentation before the evaluations." The task is what was required of the job seeker. The same applicant might explain, "It was my job to find a solution so it didn't reflect badly on our clinic or our team." The activity is what the job seeker did. "I found the previous year's documentation and asked our parent company to send another therapist and PT assistant to help make notes" provides an example.

The result is how the situation played out. The story might conclude with, "We completed the student evaluations on time and got a thank-you letter from the superintendent of schools."

Mock Interviews

Taking part in mock interviews can help candidates build their confidence, as well as fine-tune their presentations. A coworker or fellow student can serve as the pretend interviewer, but it is a good move to see if a career counselor at your university is willing to act as the interviewer. Another good idea is to use a digital camera to record the interview from the interviewer's point-of-view. When it is played back, it may show distracting movements or hand gestures that the job seeker can adjust before the actual interview.

CHAPTER Six

Becoming the Best

Every job has physical, mental, and ethical challenges. College coursework will provide guidance about proper procedures and best practices to follow. Internships, shadowing, and other physical therapy team members will "show you the ropes" in most workplaces. But questions about professionalism, ethical practices, and dealing with legal matters can test a therapist's self-esteem and personal values. In these situations, it is important to know some standards in the industry. It is also good to know where to look for more details.

Professionalism

The American Physical Therapy Association calls for physical therapists to live by a set of core values that can be summarized as "doing the right thing." Some of these values include altruism, ethics, excellence, caring, respect, and communication and accountability. Altruism is a selfless concern for the well-being of others. This means placing the needs

Physical therapists often take care of others besides their patients; they must also explain to family members how each patient is progressing in his or her recovery.

of the patient before those of the physical therapist. It can also mean providing volunteer or pro bono service to patients in financial need. Ethics is working within a set of principles that guide a person's or group's behavior. Physical therapists display excellence by striving to do the very best work. This means a PT must use the most current knowledge and techniques and stay abreast of advances in the field. Caring is expressed when PTs show concern, empathy, and consideration for the needs of others, including understanding the views of patients and other caregivers or advocating for a patient's special needs. Admiration for the work, opinions, or experience of others (including patients, their families, and others on their health care team) is a sign of respect. Physical therapists display communication skills when they are working to keep others informed of a patient's progress or notifying patients when their efforts have been effective or ineffective. Accountability can include being responsive to a patient's goals and needs, as well as asking for feedback from others.

APTA'S ADVICE

APTA also pays attention to integrity in PTs' diagnoses and treatments, calling for evidence-based practices instead of guesswork. The organization promotes an in-depth list of Five Things Physical Therapists and Patients Should Question, which spells out general practices to do or avoid in treating patients. For example, it advises avoiding the use of heating pads, electrical stimulation, ultrasound, cold packs, and other "passive physical agents" instead of active treatment techniques when treating patients. It also counsels PTs to skip the use of continuous passive motion machines for the management of patients following uncomplicated total knee replacement. APTA says such treatments add little to a patient's short- or long-term knee recovery. When treating older adults, therapists often prescribe low-dose exercise and physical activity that are physiologically inadequate to increase gains in muscle strength. APTA advises developing a strength-training plan that is tailored to help patients regain strength.

APTA goes into some detail to map out its stance on professionalism in physical therapy on its website. Similar guidelines or principles are in place for other health care professionals, and many employers in health care publish a set of core values for all employees. Taken together, these values help create a professional environment in which PTs and other team members are committed to achieving the best health and wellness in patients and the community.

Ethics in Physical Therapy

Patients and clients of physical therapists deserve to be treated with dignity, fairness, and respect. APTA has created a code of ethics that serves as a set of standards for how PTs and PTAs should behave and perform their duties. While written to help therapists behave responsibly, the code also helps educate students, other health care professionals, government regulators, and the public about the values, ethical principles, and standards expected for physical therapists.

The code states that physical therapists "shall respect the inherent dignity and rights of all individuals." This means treating all patients equally, regardless of age, gender, race, nationality, religion, ethnicity, social or economic status, or sexual orientation. The code also notes, "Physical therapists shall be trustworthy and compassionate in addressing the rights and needs of patients." This asks the therapist to always act in the best interest of the patient, and provide the information that patients and caregivers need to make thoughtful treatment choices. The words "Physical therapists shall be accountable for making sound

Trust, compassion, patience, and respect are among the many traits expected in a successful physical therapist. These behaviors make it easier to build relationships with patients.

professional judgments" call on therapists to use professional standards, evidence (current literature and established best practices), and practitioner experience when choosing a treatment plan. "Physical therapists shall demonstrate integrity in their relationships with patients/clients, families, colleagues, students, research participants, other health care providers, employers, payers, and the public" is also part of the code. This asks therapists to be truthful, not exploit patients or subordinates, and discourage and report illegal or unethical acts of other health care providers to officials.

This code of ethics shares many requirements with codes used by other health care professions. For newcomers to physical therapy, it is worthwhile to think of such ethical codes as "the rules of the road" as they navigate the profession. APTA also provides a related set of Standards of Ethical Conduct for the Physical Therapist Assistant; this document sets similar expectations as the code of ethics, but also emphasizes continued education and lifelong learning for PTAs.

Dealing with Legal Matters

Like most health care professionals, physical therapists work in situations in which health care laws, rules, and regulations must be followed. For example, today's heightened emphasis on patient privacy means a therapist who discloses personal information about a patient without that patient's consent can be fined and/or reprimanded.

When employed full-time by a hospital or health care system, a physical therapist may turn to the organization's legal department for advice regarding work-related legal issues. Self-employed physical therapists, however, need to obtain legal advice and insurance on their own, so they should budget for these expenses accordingly. Attorneys and practices that specialize in defending physical therapists from lawsuits can be found online or through networking.

Medical malpractice is a frequent concern. For example, when a patient suffers injuries because of a physical therapist's mistake, the injured patient may consider filing a physical therapy malpractice lawsuit. Malpractice suits have been filed against therapists for failure to refer a patient or consult a specialist, improper technique that may have caused injury, injury during manipulation, or equipment malfunction. Therapists can also be sued for how they run their businesses.

No one goes into a profession worried about legal action, and medical malpractice lawsuits shouldn't deter anyone from pursuing a career in physical therapy. Practices can help reduce the possibility of legal action by performing a risk management study and then reducing or eliminating risks in the practice and procedures in use.

APTA's website offers helpful guidelines in looking for an attorney with the experience and knowledge to help with your legal needs. Networking with other physical therapy professionals can also help you find an attorney who will be able to address the needs of your specific legal situation.

CHAPTER *Seven*

The Road Ahead

With promising job outlooks for physical therapists and physical therapy assistants and aides, the future looks rosy. How do students make the most of these opportunities in their communities?

Understanding trends and demands calls for looking at how people work, play, age, and raise their families—and deciding what area of specialization will be most satisfying. For example, one growing discipline within physical therapy is "work hardening." This is a form of treatment designed to help a person either return to his or her job after an injury or take a different assignment with the same employer. Regional health systems and private PT practices are recognizing this as a potential growth opportunity for employers looking to retain talented employees who become injured.

In work hardening, physical therapists work to simulate the patient's work environment. They re-create work tasks that may have contributed to the worker's pain or injury. After testing a patient's

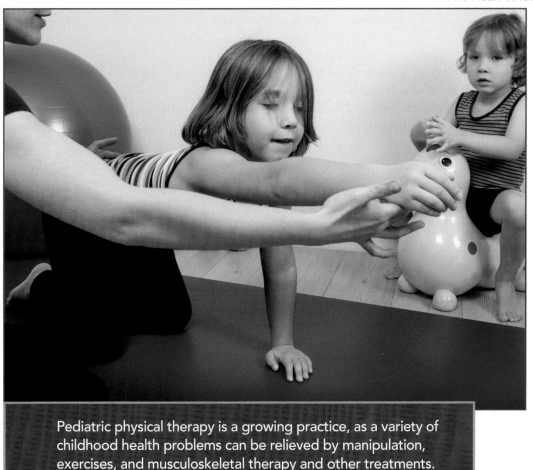

Pediatric physical therapy is a growing practice, as a variety of childhood health problems can be relieved by manipulation, exercises, and musculoskeletal therapy and other treatments.

strength and endurance, treatments usually deal with the patient's overall physical condition, strength, endurance, and coordination when performing his or her normal work activities.

What is the outlook for specialization in work hardening? In communities where manufacturing, repetitive food preparation, and physical labor are in demand, there will be a demand for physical therapists who focus on work hardening.

Another area with steady demand is pediatric physical therapy. Children face an assortment of health problems—including cerebral palsy, traumatic brain injuries, chronic pain, cancer, cystic fibrosis, and scoliosis—that call for musculoskeletal therapy and other treatments.

Dealing with the Whole Patient

Successful physical therapists quickly realize there is more to the job than clinical technique and musculoskeletal knowledge. They realize that how patients feel has as much to do with their emotional state as their physical needs.

"You deal with people in a lot of chronic pain," says Dr. Rick Kring, a physical therapist and director of clinical research at the Cleveland Clinic in Cleveland, Ohio. "That pain is keeping them from work and spending time doing things they enjoy with their families. So you're a bit of a counselor to those people. You have a goal in mind that we need to get through this sort of treatment. But patients may not be emotionally or psychologically ready to do that."

Most physicians can spend only a few minutes with each patient in order to stay on schedule. Physical therapists need to keep a different pace, Kring says. "We're typically with a patient for a half hour to an hour at a time. You have to be someone who likes to talk and listen and mingle with different ideas."

Helping people is at the heart of physical therapy. But today's many electronic distractions—including computers, smartphones, and gaming—make it tough to stay focused. Other distractions aren't electronic but may appear in the form of overprotective family members whose concerns may heighten a patient's discomfort. Physical therapists need to learn how to

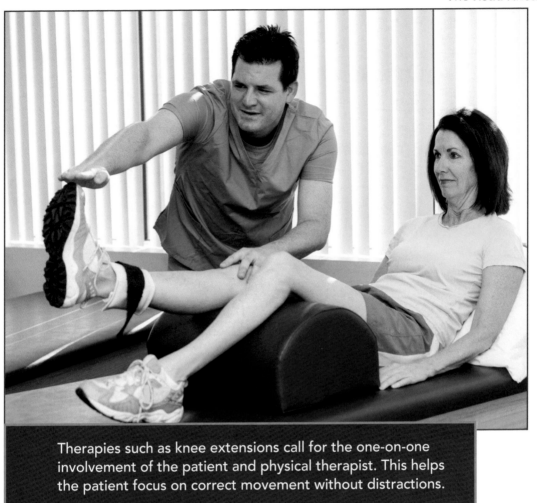

Therapies such as knee extensions call for the one-on-one involvement of the patient and physical therapist. This helps the patient focus on correct movement without distractions.

redirect family members' over-involvement and focus on the patient's concerns without a nervous parent or relative creating unneeded anxiety.

Learn to tune out such distractions when dealing with patients and health care partners. As a student completes his or her studies and pursues a PT license, it is important to develop personal interaction skills. Practice the art of listening and interacting with patients—as well as that of asking the right questions!

Creating Demand for Physical Therapy

As today's active-but-aging adult population nears retirement and leaves the workforce, it is creating demand for more physical therapy services. Changes in how all health care providers are reimbursed by Medicare and health insurance companies will affect how physical therapy practices and health care systems recruit and hire new physical therapists.

As new physical therapists consider whether to work in nursing facilities, hospitals, sports operations, or school systems, it is important to look at how insurers and government agencies change reimbursement policies or pay the company employing the physical therapist. Colleges and universities that invest heavily in strong NCAA-sanctioned athletic programs will always need trainers and physical therapists to help student-athletes strengthen and rebound from injuries. They may be less affected by the ups and downs of reimbursement changes than dedicated health care systems.

Another option is starting a private or individual physical therapy practice. This may present the option of operating as a cash-based or fee-for-service practice, in which the patient pays all the costs of his or her treatments. This model may free the practitioner from the uncertainties of Medicare and health insurer reimbursements, but it can limit the potential patient pool to only those with enough money to pay for all their care themselves.

IT'S ABOUT MARKETING, TOO

Dr. Jarod Carter, a graduate of the University of St. Augustine in Florida who practices physical therapy in Austin, Texas, says it is not enough for newly graduated therapists to have great clinical skills and professionalism. They need to sharpen their marketing abilities, too, because patients look for physical therapy information online.

"Physical therapists need to develop business and marketing skills," he says. "Like other professionals, they can use social media sites like Facebook and Twitter to promote their practice and expertise." Creating a website or Facebook page can be relatively easy. Writing or contributing to a blog about physical therapy is a good way to promote knowledge and experience, as well as to connect with others.

Most colleges' DPT degree programs emphasize diagnoses and treatment, but don't include classes in marketing, finance, or business. Carter advises that any physical therapist "become an informal student of business," taking advantage of books, publications, and online articles that offer ideas on how to grow and market a PT practice.

The More Things Change

Technology has changed the way many people live, work, and play. Digital wrist monitors track heart rate, steps walked, and other biophysical factors. The health care community offers no shortage of new innovations, right down to the digitally controlled fitness and rehab machines used by physical therapists and trainers.

But not every industry rushes to adopt the newest technologies or ergonomically designed work equipment. For example, established corporations often recycle office chairs, workstations, and other equipment after an employee leaves, instead of purchasing newer equipment with up-to-date orthopedic designs. While public schools have pursued and received technology upgrades in many communities, the desks and chairs that students use may not have changed in years. The slow pace of society's move toward safer, more ergonomic classrooms and workplaces means a steady parade of muscle strains, repetitive motion disorders, and other ailments.

Caring for Physical Therapists

Like any non-deskbound job, physical therapy can be rewarding and demanding. The road to a patient's recovery involves a physical and emotional investment. Physical therapists must warm up like athletes to prepare for a day of lifting, stretching, walking, and other muscle-stretching activities. If a patient weighs more than 300 pounds (136 kilograms), that makes for a challenging lift. Working with young children often requires the therapist to spend plenty of time on the floor, which can be hard on back muscles. Physical therapists must remember to take care of their own bodies and mental health,

Physical therapy is a demanding and satisfying career. Being a physical therapist can prove emotionally and physically tiring, but most PTs love the challenges that the job offers.

too. About one in four physical therapists chooses to work part-time, rather than full-time, to maintain a work-life balance that meets their needs for income and family time.

Yet, with all the challenges, education, licensing, and other requirements, physical therapy's rewards are hard to beat, says physical therapist Heidi Bechtold. She estimates that 80 percent of her work experiences are satisfying. She says, "You build relationships with severely injured patients, and you give them back something that they lost. It's a tremendously rewarding experience."

GLOSSARY

ACCREDITED Officially recognized as meeting the basic requirements for something.

AILMENT An illness or injury.

ANATOMY Internal physical structure of an animal or plant.

ARTHRITIS An illness that results in stiffness, pain, and swollen joints.

CEREBRAL PALSY A condition of neurological disorders that affect body movement and muscle coordination.

CHRONIC In medicine, a condition that lasts a long time or occurs often.

DEXTERITY Skill and ease at moving things, in particular the hands.

DIAGNOSIS Identifying a disease or ailment by examining a patient's signs and symptoms.

EVALUATE To study something in order to judge its condition.

GERIATRICS A branch of medicine that deals with the treatment of diseases of old age and aging.

MANIPULATION The skillful movement or handling of something in order to create a change.

MENTOR A teacher or guide.

MODALITIES Therapeutic methods such as surgery, chemotherapy, or manipulation that help physically treat a disorder.

MOTOR SKILLS A person's ability to precisely move muscles and limbs to perform a specific task.

ORTHOPEDICS An area of medicine dealing with the research and correction of deformed bones, muscles, and nerves.

OUTPATIENT Receiving medical treatment or care without admission to a hospital.

PARAPLEGIC A person who is not able to move the lower half of his or her body.

PEDIATRIC Involving the treatment of infants, children, and teenagers.

PHYSIOLOGY An area of biology that focuses on how living things function.

THERAPY Treatment intended to cure illness or injury or help relieve pain.

FOR MORE INFORMATION

American Physical Therapy Association (APTA)
1111 North Fairfax Street
Alexandria, VA 22314
(800) 999-2782 or (703) 684-2782
Website: http://www.apta.org
APTA is a national organization of eighty-eight thousand
members that works to support and enhance the
practice, research, professional standards, and
education of physical therapists in the United States.

Canadian Alliance of Physiotherapy Regulators
1243 Islington Avenue, Suite 501
Toronto, ON M8X 1Y9
Canada
(416) 234-8800
Website: http://www.alliancept.org
The Alliance is the pan-Canadian federation of
provincial/territorial physiotherapy regulators
committed to the development and improvement
of regulatory standards of practice for
physiotherapists.

Canadian Physiotherapy Association (CPA)
955 Green Valley Crescent, Suite 270
Ottawa, ON K2C 3V4
Canada
(613) 564-5454 or (800) 387-8679
Website: http://www.physiotherapy.ca
The CPA represents some twelve thousand physiotherapy professionals and students across Canada. The group is dedicated to the health, mobility,
and fitness of Canadians and provides information
for therapists and the public.

Federation of State Boards of Physical Therapy
    (FSBPT)
124 West Street South, 3rd Floor
Alexandria, VA 22314
(703) 299-3100
Website: http://www.fsbpt.org
This member-driven organization provides information to
    the public about physical therapy basics, how to find
    a licensed physical therapist, and patients' rights.

Sports Physical Therapy Section (SPTS)
9002 N. Meridian Street, Suite 112A
Indianapolis, IN 46260
(877) 732-5009
Website: http://www.spts.org
Founded in 1973, SPTS is a component member of
    the American Physical Therapy Association that
    provides a forum for members of the association
    with an interest in sports physical therapy and
    athletic trainers.

Websites

Because of the changing nature of Internet links,
Rosen Publishing has developed an online list of
websites related to the subject of this book. This site
is updated regularly. Please use this link to access
the list:

http://www.rosenlinks.com/CIYC/Phys

Andrews, James, Gary Harrelson, and Kevin Wilk. *Physical Rehabilitation of the Injured Athlete: Expert Consult*. Philadelphia, PA: Saunders/Elsevier, 2012.

Brezina, Corona. *Getting a Job in Health Care*. New York, NY: Rosen Publishing, 2013.

Combs, Melissa. *How to Land a Top-Paying Physical Therapy Assistants Job: Your Complete Guide to Opportunities, Resumes and Cover Letters, Interviews, Salaries, Promotions, What to Expect from Recruiters and More*. Newstead, Australia: Emereo Pty Limited, 2012.

Flath, Camden. *Therapy Jobs in Educational Settings: Speech, Physical, Occupational, & Audiology*. Broomall, PA: Mason Crest Publishers, 2010.

Franklin, Delia. *Nursing Homes Explained*. New York, NY: Algora Publishing, 2013.

Garner, Geraldine. *Careers in Social and Rehabilitation Services*. New York, NY: McGraw-Hill, 2008.

Guiliana, John, Hal Ornstein, and Mark Terry. *31 1/2 Essentials for Running Your Medical Practice*. Phoenix, MD: Greenbranch Publishing, 2010.

Harasymiw, Therese. *A Career as a Physical Therapist* (Essential Careers). New York, NY: Rosen Publishing, 2011.

John-Nwankwo, Jane. *Choosing a Healthcare Career: Becoming a Healthcare Professional*. Seattle, WA: CreateSpace/On-Demand Publishing, 2013.

Kenney, W. Larry, Jack Wilmore, and David Costill. *Physiology of Sport and Exercise with Web Study Guide*. 5th ed. Windsor, ON, Canada: Human Kinetics, 2011.

Levine, Adele. *Run, Don't Walk: The Curious and Chaotic Life of a Physical Therapist Inside Walter Reed Army Medical Center*. New York, NY: Avery/Penguin Group, 2014.

McClusky, Mark. *Faster, Higher, Stronger: How Sports Science Is Creating a New Generation of Superathletes—and What We Can Learn from Them*. New York, NY: Hudson Street Press/ Penguin Group, 2014.

O'Sullivan, Susan B. *National Physical Therapy Examination: Review & Study Guide 2013*. Evanston, IL: Therapyed, 2012.

Painter, Kirk G. *So You Want to Be a Therapist? How to Become a Physical or Occupational Therapist*. Seattle, WA: CreateSpace/On-Demand Publishing, 2013.

Schuman, Nancy, and Burton Jay Nadler. *1,001 Phrases You Need to Get a Job: The "Hire Me" Words That Set Your Cover Letter, Resume, and Job Interview Apart*. Avon, MA: Adams Media Corp., 2012.

Sing, Patrick. *Health Care in Canada Including Government Involvement, Private Sector, and Medical Organizations*. Webster's Digital Services, 2012.

Walker, Richard. *The Human Machine: An Owner's Guide to the Body*. New York, NY: Oxford University Press, 2008.

Wischnitzer, Edith, and Saul Wischnitzer. *Top 100 Health-Care Careers*. St. Paul, MN: JIST Publishing, 2010.

BIBLIOGRAPHY

"Graduate Schools for Physical Therapy." *U.S. News & World Report*, 2012. Retrieved November 2, 2014 (http://grad-schools.usnews.rankingsandreviews. com/best-graduate-schools/top-health-schools/ physical-therapy-rankings?int=983208).

American Academy of Orthopaedic Surgeons. "The Burden of Musculoskeletal Disease." 2008. Retrieved November 8, 2014 (http://www.boneandjointburden .org/pdfs/bmus_executive_summary_low.pdf).

American Physical Therapists Association. "Code of Ethics for the Physical Therapist." June 21, 2010. Retrieved November 24, 2014 (http://www.apta.org /uploadedFiles/APTAorg/About_Us/Policies/HOD /Ethics/CodeofEthics.pdf)

American Physical Therapists Association. "Five Things Physical Therapists and Patients Should Question." September 15, 2014. Retrieved October 29, 2014 (http://www.choosingwisely.org/doctor-patient-lists/ american-physical-therapy-association).

Bunn, Laura. "What Percentage of Physical Therapists Are Women?" eHow/Demand Media. Retrieved October 28, 2014 (http://www.ehow.com/ about_5568437_percentage-physical-therapists- women.html).

Bureau of Labor Statistics, U.S. Department of Labor. "Physical Therapists." *Occupational Outlook Handbook*, 2014-15 Edition, January 8, 2014. Retrieved November 5, 2014 (http://www.bls.gov/ ooh/healthcare/physical-therapists.htm).

Carter, Jarod. "Important Info for Physical Therapy Students—Things to Know Before Graduation." August 4, 2012. Retrieved November 2, 2014 (https://www.youtube.com/ watch?v=BZpYTZWTj5U).

Center for Integrity in Practice. "Choosing Wisely: The Right Care at the Right Time." September 26, 2014. Retrieved October 30, 2014 (http://integrity.apta.org /ChoosingWisely).

Forces.ca. "Physiotherapy Officer." Retrieved November 6, 2014 (http://www.forces.ca/en/job/ physiotherapyofficer-44).

GoArmy.com. "Physical Therapist." Retrieved November 5, 2014 (http://www.goarmy.com/careers- and-jobs/amedd-categories/medical-specialist- corps-jobs/physical-therapist.html).

"Graduate Schools for Physical Therapy." *U.S. News & World Report*. 2012. Retrieved November 2, 2014 (http://grad-schools.usnews .rankingsandreviews.com/best-graduate- schools/top-healthschools/physical-therapy- rankings?int=983208).

Gurnick, Ken. "At Top of Her Field, Falsone Humbled by Attention." MLB.com, March 12, 2012. Retrieved October 28, 2014 (http://mlb.mlb.com/news/print .jsp?ymd=20120312&content_id=27222246&c_ id=mlb).

Harasymiw, Therese. *A Career as a Physical Therapist* (Essential Careers). New York, NY: Rosen Publishing, 2011.

Higgins, Michael. "Using the Star Technique to Shine at Job Interviews: A How-to Guide." *Guardian*, March 10, 2014. Retrieved November 1, 2014 (http://careers.theguardian.com/careers-blog/star- technique-competency-based-interview).

Kring, Rick. "How to Become a Physical Therapist." TheCareerZoo.com, July 17, 2013. Retrieved November 2, 2014 (https://www.youtube.com/ watch?v=S7uOyq7G4KM).

Lantz, Ryan. "Therapy in Film." Advanced-medical.com, June 22, 2011. Retrieved October 29, 2014 (http://www.advanced-medical.net/occupational-therapy/therapy-film).

Machlin, Steven R., Julia Chevan, William W. Yu, and Marc W. Zodet. "Determinants of Utilization and Expenditures for Episodes of Ambulatory Physical Therapy Among Adults." *Physical Therapy Journal*, July 2011. Retrieved November 1, 2014 (http://www.physicaltherapyjournal.com/content/91/7/1018.full).

Mangusan, David, Jr. "Canada Physiotherapy Schools—List of Canadian Physiotherapy Schools." 2011. Retrieved November 2, 2014 (http://www.physiotherapynotes.com/2011/03/canada-physiotherapy-schools-list-of.html).

Mosby. *Mosby's Medical Dictionary*, 8th ed. New York, NY: Elsevier Health, 2009.

PhysiotherapyEducation.ca. "2014 Canadian Council of Physiotherapy University Programs." Retrieved November 2, 2014 (http://www.physiotherapyeducation.ca/CanadianPrograms.html).

Sports Physical Therapy Section. "Physical Therapists Added to NFL Team Medical Staffs." Retrieved November 1, 2014 (http://spts.org).

Stern, David T. *Measuring Medical Professionalism*. New York, NY: Oxford University Press, 2006.

Wisconsin Department of Public Instruction. "School Based Physical Therapy." Retrieved November 3, 2014 (http://sped. dpi.wi.gov/sped_phy-ther).

About the Author

David Kassnoff is a communications professional, writer, and educator with more than twenty years' experience working with information technology and health care professionals and executives in corporate and not-for-profit organizations. His writing has appeared in many mainstream and industry publications, including *American Biotechnology Laboratory*, *Diversity Executive*, *Profiles in Diversity Journal*, *USA Weekend*, *Audio-Visual Communications*, Gannett Rochester Newspapers, *Photo Marketing*, *Rochester Business*, *Los Angeles Times Magazine*, *Photo Trade News*, and *Practical Homeowner*. He also teaches at the Russell J. Jandoli School of Journalism and Mass Communication at St. Bonaventure University. His work has been recognized for excellence by the New York State Newspaper Publishers Association and the Council for Advancement and Support of Education.

Photo Credits

Cover, p. 33 © iStockphoto.com/Steve Debenport; pp. 5, 17, 54, 63 © iStockphoto.com/Kali Nine LLC; p. 9 T-Design/Shutterstock.com; p. 11 © AP Images; p. 13 Keith Brofsky/Photodisc/Thinkstock; p. 19 Frank Pedrick/Photolibrary/Getty Images; p. 22 Hemera Technologies/AbleStock.com/Thinkstock; p. 25 Tyler Olson/Shutterstock.com; p. 27 Spencer Grant/Photo Researchers, Inc./Science Source; p. 31 © iStockphoto.com/sturti; p. 35 Don Bayley/iStock/Thinkstock; p. 38 U.S. Army; p. 43 Daniel Korzeniewski/Shutterstock.com; p. 45 Fuse/Thinkstock; p. 49 Spencer Platt/Getty Images; p. 50 racorn/Shutterstock.com; p. 57 © iStockphoto.com/Pamela Moore; p. 61 purplequeue/Shutterstock.com; p. 67 © iStockphoto.com/DNY59; cover and interior pages border and background images © iStockphoto.com/galdzer (skeleton), © iStockphoto.com/Pingebat (map).

Designer: Nicole Russo; Editor: Amelie von Zumbusch